HOW TO BE A Jewish Mother

A Very Lovely Training Manual

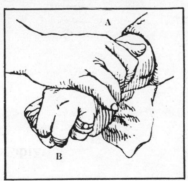

By Dan Greenburg

PRICE/STERN/SLOAN
Publishers, Inc., Los Angeles

ILLUSTRATIONS BY GERRY GERSTEN
COVER BY TONY PALLADINO
DESIGN AND PRODUCTION BY JOHN LIPARI AND DAN GREENBURG
PHOTOGRAPHS BY SAM GREENBURG
TECHNICAL ASSISTANCE BY MRS LEAH GREENBURG
AUTHOR'S YOUNGER SISTER PLAYED BY NAOMI GREENBURG

Published by Price/Stern/Sloan Publishers, Inc.
410 North La Cienega Blvd., Los Angeles, California 90048
Copyright© 1964, 1965, 1972, 1975 by Dan Greenburg
Printed in the United States of America. All Rights Reserved
Library of Congress Catalog Card Number: 64-56430
ISBN: 0-8431-0030-3

Eighth Printing—March 1979

What This Book Will Teach You

VIII. *The Jewish Mother's Guide to Sex and Marriage (Page 65)*

Foreword by the Author's Mother

I just wanted to tell you that this book was written by my son who is a very capable young man. I haven't actually read what he has to say here but I'm sure it's very pleasant if he wrote it. You'd think that it wouldn't be such a hardship on a young man who writes so nicely to write an occasional letter to his mother who loves him, but it seems there are more important things to a young man these days than his mother. All right, never mind. I only hope you will like the book and I pray that the whole experience has taught him something.

I.
The Basic Techniques of Jewish Motherhood

The Basic Theory

There is more to being a Jewish Mother than being Jewish and a mother.[1] Properly practiced, Jewish motherhood is an art—a complex network of subtle and highly sophisticated techniques.

Master these techniques and you will be an unqualified success—the envy of your friends and the backbone of your family.

Fail to master these techniques and you hasten the black day you discover your children can get along without you.

---

[1] On the other hand, you don't have to be either Jewish or a mother to be a Jewish mother. An Irish waitress or an Italian barber could also be a Jewish mother.

Basic Philosophizing

You will be called upon to function as a philosopher on two distinct types of occasions:

(1) Whenever anything bad happens.
(2) Whenever anything good happens.

Whenever anything bad happens, you must point out the fortunate aspects of the situation:

> "Ma! Ma!"
> "What's the commotion?"
> "The bad boys ran off with my hat!"
> "The bad boys ran off with your hat? You should be grateful they didn't also cut your throat."

Also point out that Bad Experience is the best teacher:

> "Maybe next time you'll know better than to fool with roughnecks.[2] It's the best thing that could have happened to you, believe me."

Whenever anything good happens, you must, of course, point out the unfortunate aspects of the

[2]See glossary.

situation. (This is necessary in order that The Evil Eye should not suspect that things are going too well):

>"Ma! Ma!"
>
>"So what's the trouble now?"
>
>"The Youth Group Raffle! I won a Pontiac convertible!"
>
>"You won a Pontiac automobile in the Youth Group Raffle? Very nice. The insurance alone is going to send us to the poorhouse."

Making Guilt Work

Underlying all techniques of Jewish Motherhood is the ability to plant, cultivate and harvest guilt. Control guilt and you control the child.

An old folk saw says "Beat a child every day; if you don't know what he's done to deserve the beating, <u>he</u> will." A slight modification gives us the Jewish Mother's cardinal rule:

Let your child hear you sigh' every day; if you don't know what he's done to make you suffer, <u>he</u> will.

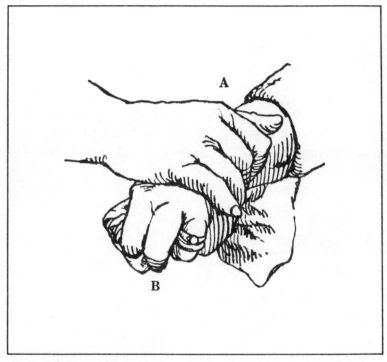

FIG. I: PROPER POSITION OF HANDS DURING EXECUTION OF DAILY SIGH.

Note: **(A)** Cross-Over Grip of Right Hand on Left Wrist, **(B)** Edge of Plain Linen Handkerchief tucked around Index Finger to facilitate tear-dabbing.

The Technique of Basic Suffering

To master the Technique of Basic Suffering you should begin with an intensive study of the Dristan commercials on television. Pay particular attention to the face of the actor who has not yet taken Dristan.

Note the squint of the eyes, the furrow of the brow, the downward curve of the lips—the pained expression which can only come from eight undrained sinus cavities or severe gastritis.

This is the Basic Facial Expression. Learn it well. Practice it before a mirror several times a day. If someone should catch you at it and ask what you are doing, say:

"I'm fine, it's nothing at all, it will go away."

This should be said softly but audibly, should imply suffering without expressing it openly. When properly executed, this is the Basic Tone of Voice.

Practice Drills

(1) Give your son Marvin two sportshirts as a present. The first time he wears one of them, look at him sadly and say in your Basic Tone of Voice: "The other one you didn't like?"

(2) Borrow a tape recorder and practice the following key phrases until you can deliver them with eye-watering perfection:

> (a) "Go ahead and enjoy yourself."
> (b) "But be careful."
> (c) "Don't worry about me."
> (d) "I don't mind staying home alone."
> (e) "I'm glad it happened to me and not to you."

(3) Remember, the child is an unformed, emotionally unstable, ignorant creature. To make him feel secure, you must continually remind him of the things which you are denying yourself on his account, especially when others are present.

Seven Basic Sacrifices To Make For Your Child

(1) Stay up all night to prepare him a big breakfast.

(2) Go without lunch so you can put an extra apple in his lunchpail.

(3) Give up an evening of work with a charitable institution so that he can have the car on a date.

(4) Tolerate the girl he's dating.

(5) Don't let him know you fainted twice in the supermarket from fatigue. (But make sure he knows you're not letting him know.)

(6) When he comes home from the dentist, take over his toothache for him.

(7) Open his bedroom window wider so he can have more fresh air, and close your own so you don't use up the supply.

Now that you have familiarized yourself with the Basic Techniques, you may proceed to apply this knowledge in the important area of Food Distribution.

II.
The Jewish Mother's Guide to Food Distribution

Just as Mother Nature abhors a vacuum, the Jewish Mother abhors an empty mouth. It shall therefore be your purpose as a Jewish Mother to fill every mouth you can reach with nourishing food.

Mealtime Strategy: First and Second Helpings

At mealtimes, be sure there is a continuous flow of food from stove to serving platter to plate to mouth. If anyone should be foolish enough to decline a particular dish (e.g. potatoes), proceed as follows:

(1) Find out whether the man has any rational objections:

"What do you <u>mean</u> no potatoes, Irving —you think I'm trying to poison you?"

(2) Suggest that he take only a small amount as a compromise:

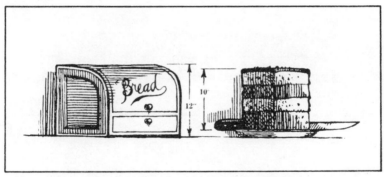

FIG. II: DIAGRAM INDICATING PROPER INTERPRETATION OF THE PHRASE "SLIVER OF FOOD."

"Take only a <u>sliver</u> of the potatoes, then."

"All right. But remember, only a sliver."

(3) You may now proceed to fill his plate with potatoes. The instant he has crammed down the last one, you must be ready to:

(4) Offer him a second helping:

"There, I told you you'd like it once you tasted it. All right now, you're ready for seconds?"

"God, no."

Here you must really be on your toes. Between your question and his answer, little more than one microsecond will elapse. Within that microsecond, you must scoop all the rest of the potatoes out onto his plate and make the turn back to the kitchen. If you either scoop too soon or scoop too late, you risk a serious breach of sportsmanship. The scooping motion must come precisely between your "—ready for seconds?" and his "God, no." A few hours of

FIG. III: PROPER FORM FOR ADMINISTERING THE SECOND HELPING.

(1) The Staging Phase: Right Hand (A), grips Kettle (B), while Left Hand (C) holds Ladle (D) in a firm but comfortable grip. (2) The Pre-Contactual Phase: Note the snap of the Wrist, the angle of the plane of the Ladle Top. (3) The Post-Contactual Phase: Between this and the preceding phase is the Moment of Truth; it must occur precisely between your "... seconds?" and the target's "God, no." (4) The Follow-Through Phase: Consistent form is realized by bringing the Ladle sharply upward and in position to return to the Kettle for the Third Helping.

practice with a stopwatch in the privacy of your kitchen should net you surprisingly satisfactory results.[3]

Bread With Everything

Never forget the importance of bread in the diet. Urge that it be eaten with all foods, even snacks:

> "Irving, wait. Take a little bread with that."
> "Bread? With strawberry ice cream?"
> "Just a little piece. To help wash it down."

How To Administer The Third Helping

When the last crumb has been cleared from all plates by means of vague references to privation in Europe, you are ready for the real test of your art. Begin with a general all-inclusive warning:

> "I am now ready to begin serving third helpings."

---

[3]Until your timing has been perfected, it is perhaps slightly better form to scoop too early than to have his "God, no" catch you with your potatoes halfway down.

Immediately switch from the general to the specific. Select your quarry, and pounce:

> "Eddie, I can tell you are ready for a third helping of chicken."
> "Believe me, Sylvia, if I took one more piece of chicken I would sprout feathers."

The next step in the ritual calls for a statement about your quarry addressed to the spectators:

> "Eddie doesn't like the way I cook chicken."
> "I'm crazy about the way you cook chicken, Sylvia. I simply cannot eat another particle without bursting."
> "You see, I happen to know that chicken is Eddie's favorite dish. I prepared it specially for him—but do you think he cares?"

Note that in this exchange your remarks are not <u>to</u> Eddie but <u>about</u> him.[4] You are now ready to close in for the moment of truth:

[4]See THE THIRD PERSON INVISIBLE, Page 70.

"Eddie, tell me. You like chicken?"

"Yes."

"You like <u>my</u> chicken?"

"Yes yes."

"You are too full to eat any more?"

"Yes yes yes."

"All right. This I can understand. A man says to me 'I am too full', this I can understand. It's not like you are asking me to throw it out, after all. All right. (PAUSE) So I'll wrap it up in wax paper and you'll take it for later."

Watch Between-Meal-Treats

Between meals, follow guests about the house with trays of fruit, nuts, candies, cookies, cakes and sour pickles. Eating should never be restricted to the dining table, particularly if there is some question of health involved:

"Marvin, how about a little treat? Have a mint, or maybe a slice of salami."

"Not now, Ma."

"Have a grape, or a nice watermelon. You want me to slice you a watermelon?"

"I said not <u>now,</u> Ma!"

"Listen how he talks to me. You'd think I was trying to do a terrible thing to him, to slice him a watermelon. Do you see how skinny he is? A scarecrow. Look at him—you'd think I never gave him a decent meal in his life. Tuberculosis—that's what he'll get. Then he'll eat. They'll feed him through a tube."

"Aw, for crynoutloud. Give me the watermelon already."

"Here. Enjoy it. You'll learn how to eat some day, but by then—God forbid—it will be too late."[5]

---

[5]Should your child ever leave home, temporarily or permanently, do not let him go without giving him a bag of sandwiches. At last report, they were still selling food on The Outside, but they are liable to stop at any moment. And besides, how good can it be?

Matching Test

Match the main dish in Column I with its appropriate side dish in Column II:

I	II
(1) Roast brisket of beef	(a) Celery
(2) Boiled chicken	(b) Tomato
(3) Fried chicken	(c) Lettuce
(4) Turkey	(d) String beans
(5) Macaroni	(e) Carrots
(6) Veal cutlets	(f) Peas
(7) Rib steak	(g) Beets
(8) Lamb chops	(h) Spinach
(9) Beef stew	(i) Bread
(10) Pressed duck	(j) Corn

Answers

(1) i
(2) i
(3) i
(4) i
(5) i
(6) i
(7) i
(8) i
(9) i
(10) i

You now know how to effectively Distribute Food. Next you will learn how to Entertain.

III.
The Jewish Mother's Guide to Entertaining

Your job as hostess is not complete when your guests have been properly fed. You must see to it that they are also entertained. Here are a few excellent suggestions for after-dinner entertainment:

8:30—Have your son play the violin.

9:00—Have your daughter play the piano.

9:30—Have your daughter show what she learned in tap dancing class.

9:45—Have your son read a composition that should have gotten a better grade.

10:00—Tell a funny story.

How to Tell a Funny Story

Your family and friends will expect you to be able to relate amusing stories which you have heard at the butcher shop, at a meeting of Hadassah, or which your husband has told at a previous gathering of these same people. Familiarize yourself with the following formula for successful story telling and in no time at all you will have a widespread reputation as a raconteuse. To begin the telling of any story:

(1) Ask whether anybody has heard it before.

"Listen, you all know the story about the old Jewish man?"

It is important that this initial query be as general as possible, so that anybody who has heard the story before should not recognize it and hence have it spoiled for him. The next step is:

(2) Ask someone else to tell it.

"Listen, it's a very funny story. About an old Jewish man. Al, you tell it."

"I don't know the story you mean, Sylvia."

"Of course you know. Don't you? The story about the old Jewish man. Go ahead, you tell it, Al. You know I can't tell a story properly."

This modesty is very becoming to a performer and will surely be countered with heartfelt cries of denial from your audience. You are now ready to:

(3) Explain Where You Heard the Story.

"All right. This story I heard originally from Rose Melnick. You all know Rose? No? Her husband is in dry goods. Melnick. You know the one? All right, it doesn't matter to the story, believe me. Anyway, Rose Melnick heard it from her son-in-law, Seymour, a lovely boy, really. A nose and throat man. Seymour Rosen— you know the name?"

By now your audience has been sufficiently prepared for the story and will be anxious for you to begin. Go ahead and tell it, but be sure to:

(4) Begin the Story at the Ending.

Professional comedians call the end of the story "the punch line". Since this is usually the funniest part of the story, it is logically the best place to start:

"Anyway, there's this old Jewish man who is trying to get into the synagogue during the Yom Kippur service, and the usher finally says to him, 'All right, go ahead in, but don't let me catch you praying.' (PAUSE) Oh, did I mention that the old man just wants to go in and give a message to somebody in the synagogue? He doesn't actually want to go into the synagogue and <u>pray</u>, you see. (PAUSE. FROWN) Wait a minute. I don't know if I mentioned that the old man doesn't have a ticket for the service. You know how crowded it always is on Yom Kippur, and the old man doesn't have a ticket, and he explains to the usher that he has to go into the synagogue and tell somebody something, but the usher isn't going to let him in without a ticket. So the old man explains to him that it's a matter of life and death, so then the usher thinks it over and he says to the old man, 'All right, go ahead in, but don't let me catch you praying.' (PAUSE. FROWN. STAND AND BEGIN EMPTYING ASHTRAYS) Ach, I don't think I told it right, Al, <u>you</u> tell it."

How to Discuss Current Events

Aside from a meeting of the Cousins Club,[6] when it is perfectly proper to limit discussion to those members of the family that could not attend the meeting, you will probably be expected to discuss Current Events, particularly when men are present. Men do not consider the prevailing price of rib roast or the progress of your niece Edith's pregnancy to be Current Events. Therefore, learn to speak their language. Memorize the following list of subjects and approved reactions and you will be well on your way to a reputation as a Well-Informed Hostess.

Fidel Castro:
A man that cannot take the trouble to shave, comb his hair and put on a suit and a clean shirt, would not get my vote, I can tell you that much.

[6]See glossary.

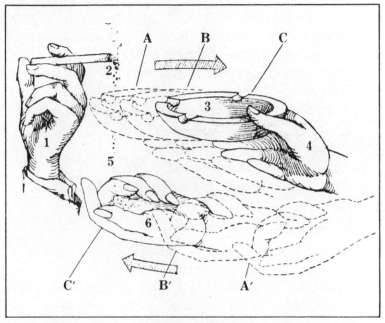

FIG. IV: PROPER FORM FOR EMPTYING ASHTRAYS WHEN ENTERTAINING.

Important: As Guest (1) begins to flick Ash (2) into Ashtray (3), your Right Hand (4) must withdraw Ashtray from Ash Drop Line (5), permitting Flicked Ash to fall into your cupped Left Hand (6). Phases of Right Hand Withdrawal, labelled A, B and C, correspond with phases of Left Hand Advance, labelled A′, B′ and C′. (Note: When Flicked Ash has been successfully caught in cupped hand, you may remark "That's all right, don't worry about it.")

Ralph Nader:
Lovely. A smart, serious person with a head on his shoulders, and not with long hair either. Wears a suit and a tie, not like some people I could mention. Lives simply and nicely, without the fancy frills. Listen, I'd be calling him ten times a week with names of lovely girls, but I understand he doesn't have a phone.

Polaris:
Something for the mouth, I think. I don't know too much about it, to tell you the truth.

Astronauts:
This is a way to earn a living? That a young man should spend all his time cooped up in a tiny cramped space without fresh air, without proper exercise, without a nourishing hot meal? Feh!

Landing on Moon:
What have they found up there that they can't get down here?

Yuri Gagarin:
Very nice. I saw him with the Bolshoi last time. Dances nice, not like a sissy.

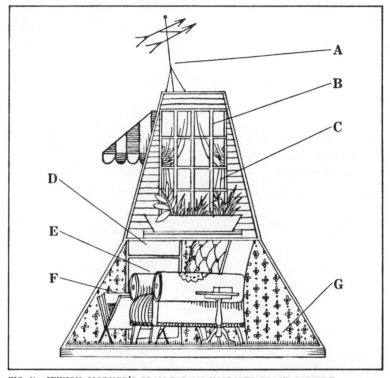

FIG. V: JEWISH MOTHER'S PLAN FOR AN IMPROVED SPACE CAPSULE.

(A) A little TV to while away the time. (B) Windows for plenty of fresh air. (C) Curtains so there shouldn't be a glare closer to the sun. (D) A nice frigidaire with plenty of cold cuts, milk and fruit. (E) A comfy chair which won't give you a curvature of the spine. (F) Some worthwhile magazines. (G) Thick wall-to-wall carpet to reduce landing shock.

Gerald Ford:
Makes a nice appearance. Very clean. He should go far.

Nelson Rockefeller:
A man that wealthy does not need to be President.

The Common Market:
I go mainly to the A & P.

Thermonuclear war:
Feh! Who needs it?

Henry Kissinger:
Listen, I know he has to talk with the Arabs -- it's his job. But it seems to me he enjoys it maybe a little too much, you know what I mean?

Pollution:
If Harry would stop smoking cigars for a minute, you could maybe get the smell out of the draperies.

Alice Cooper:
I don't understand this -- a man with the name of a lady? Maybe he is a sissy.

Mary Tyler Moore:
A nice girl. Maybe she will take a leaf from Rhoda and find herself a suitable husband before it's too late.

ICBM:
They tell me pretty soon you'll put a punched card in a machine and it will cook you a meal. Will it also darn your socks?

Sammy Davis, Jr.:
I understand he ran out and became a Jew. Listen, I give the man a lot of credit. I, myself, would not have the courage to run out and become a colored person.

Frank Sinatra:
Formerly a scarecrow. Look how nice he eats now.

Audrey Hepburn:
Put a little flesh on her and she'd be a capable girl.

Henry Miller:
I liked particularly "Death of a Salesman." His other stuff I don't understand.

Gay Liberation:
If I would be liberated from housework and have a little time to myself, believe me I would be jolly and gay. This is what you're talking about?

Dr. Spock:
Spock, shlock, don't talk to me about that stuff. A man doesn't know how to bring up children until he's been a mother.

Leonard Bernstein:
Ah! That young man is a gentleman. You can tell what kind of a home he came from.

Extrasensory perception:
Very nice.

TV dinners:
Not enough to fill even a sparrow.

Merrill Lynch, Pierce, Fenner & Smith:
Nice boys. Mike Douglas had them on last week.

The Cincinnati Reds:
In any large city you're going to find trouble-makers.

Any subject not listed above and not directly related to a profession, the household, or the care of a family you may dismiss as "A lot of foolishness."

Naturally, if you're going to do any entertaining, you're going to have to know how to pay and accept compliments.

How To Pay A Compliment

Paying people compliments is really a lot of foolishness because it either embarrasses them or gives them a swelled head. It is permissible, however, to pay a compliment in an emergency:

"Florence, what have you done to your hair? It looks like you're wearing a wig!"
"I am. All my hair fell out."
"Oh. Listen, it looks so natural I'd never have known."

How To Accept A Compliment

Never accept a compliment:

"Irving, tell me how is the chopped liver?"

"Mmmm! Sylvia, it's delicious!"

"I don't know. First the chicken livers that the butcher gave me were dry. Then the timer on the oven didn't work. Then at the last minute I ran out of onions. Tell me, how could it be good?"

Test Problem

How do you get your son to play the violin for company solely through the application of guilt?

Solution

In front of your guests, tell him you only spent all that money on lessons so he could make himself and others happy through beautiful music.

You have learned how to Distribute Food and how to Entertain. Next you must learn how to Relax.

IV.
The Jewish Mother's Guide to Relaxation

The fact that you are a Jewish Mother does not necessarily mean you can never relax. On the contrary, unless you deliberately set aside a little time for regular relaxation, you will not be able to efficiently care for your family. Therefore, plan to relax a minimum of an hour and a half every fifteen years.

How to Enjoy Yourself at Home If There Are Others Present:

Drink a little glass of cream soda and watch Johnny Carson. Or:
Listen to an Al Jolson record. Or:
Have a piece candy. Or:
Take off your shoes.

How to Enjoy Yourself at Home If There is Nobody Present:

Take off your girdle.

How to Enjoy Yourself at Home
If There is Nobody Present But Your Husband:

(1) Put on an Al Jolson record.

(2) Fix him a little glass of cream soda and a piece candy.

(3) Have him lie down and make himself comfortable on the sofa.

(4) Give him a little kiss on the top of the head.

(5) Give him a little hug around the neck.

(6) Take off your girdle.

(7) Help him take off his clothes.

(8) Iron a fresh crease in his trousers.

How to Enjoy Yourself at Somebody Else's Home:

Take your family to the home of a friend for dinner. Sit back and relax while somebody else does the cooking for a change. (But bring over something in a casserole dish and insist on serving the food, clearing the table and washing and drying the dishes.)

How to Enjoy Yourself at the Beach

Pack a basket lunch with chicken, spinach, corned beef, potato salad, tomatoes, bread, spongecake, carrots, seltzer in a thermos, celery, meat loaf, cookies, potato chips, pickles, pretzels, tuna salad sandwiches—all wrapped in aluminum foil. Distribute these to all members of the family,[7] smoothe out the aluminum foil which was wrapped around the food and fit it over a piece of cardboard to make a sun reflector. Prop this reflector against your knees so as to obtain an even suntan under your chin.

Take along plenty of suntan oil. Be sure everybody has sunglasses, with a little piece of newspaper between the lenses to protect the nose, and any kind of a hat to protect the head, and long sleeves and trousers to protect the arms and legs from sunstroke.

Don't let anybody go into the water less than four hours after eating. Caution them not to stay in the water until their lips turn blue (have them

[7] For proper techniques of food distribution see THE JEWISH MOTHER'S GUIDE TO FOOD DISTRIBUTION.

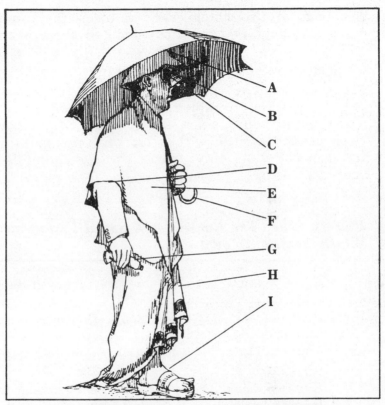

FIG. VI: PROPER OUTFIT FOR TAKING A LITTLE SUN AT THE BEACH.

(A) Something for the head to prevent sunstroke. **(B)** Something for the nose to prevent peeling. **(C)** Dark glasses for the eyes to prevent blindness. **(D)** Long-sleeved jacket to protect the arms. **(E)** Shawl to protect the jacket. **(F)** Umbrella to protect the shawl. **(G)** Cocoa butter. **(H)** Tablecloth to protect the legs from a draft. **(I)** Shower clogs to prevent the feet from picking up somebody's athlete's foot from the sand.

come out of the water every so often for you to check the color of their lips) and tell them not to go out too far. (Above the waist is too far. They could accidentally trip on a rock and drown.)

After a little coaxing from your family, announce that you are going "bathing," wade into the water up to your ankles, squeal that it's too cold, wash around a little with a bar of Ivory, splash a few drops of water on your bosom and exclaim: "Ah, such a pleasure!"

How To Leave The House For A Social Engagement Which Begins At 8:00 P.M.

7:55—Wait until the whole family is dressed and ready to go before you begin to get ready.

8:05—Tell everybody that the reason you aren't ready is that you had to supervise their getting ready.

8:40—Have somebody zip you up while you wash the last few dishes in the sink.

8:57—Call the hostess on the telephone to say you'll be a couple of minutes late because you had to supervise everybody's getting ready and because you had no help, as usual, with the dishes.

FIG. VII: APPROPRIATE WATER LEVELS FOR MAJOR BEACH ACTIVITIES.

(Level 1): Optimum Cooling Off Depth. **(Level 2):** Optimum Splashing Around Depth. **(Level 3):** Optimum Wading Depth. **(Level 4):** Maximum Allowable Swimming Depth. **(Level 5):** Certain Drowning Depth.

9:05—Go through the house turning off all the lights.

9:13—Go back and turn a few lights on in the back of the house and a few in front to make prospective burglars think there is somebody at home.

9:20—Herd everybody out of the house, double lock the door behind you, and start down the stairs, pointing out how late it is.

9:21—Rush back inside to check whether the water in the bathtub was turned off.

9:27—Double lock the door again and leave, this time getting as far as the car.

9:30—Run back upstairs to check whether all the gas jets were turned off.

9:36—Run back downstairs to the car.

9:38—Wonder whether you remembered to double lock the door this time.

9:40—Walk back upstairs and check the door.

9:45—Walk back downstairs, lean against the car, assume your Basic Facial Expression, mop your brow, and say in your Basic Tone of Voice: "Listen, why don't you kids go ahead without me. All this rushing around has made me a little faint."

Test Problem

Think of a way to make your child help you out in the kitchen so you can occasionally sit down for five minutes.

Solution

Say to him in the presence of at least three other people:

> "So how come Naomi's boy not only sets the table without being told, he also has dinner waiting when his mother comes back from shopping?"

This is known as The Neighbor's-Model-Child Gambit.

Once you have mastered the art of Relaxation you may push on to the tiring but vital area of thrift.

V.
The Jewish Mother's Guide to Thrift

Sale Merchandise Costs Less

Economy is so important you must spare no expense to achieve it. Therefore, remember these two important maxims:

(1) Never buy anything that is not on sale.

(2) Never <u>fail</u> to buy anything that <u>is</u> on sale.

Needless to say, you must never sacrifice quality for the sake of economy. A good way to check the quality of sale merchandise is to ask the merchant:

"Tell me, mister, is this a good piece
of rib steak?"

"Yeah, lady."

IMPORTANT: <u>If he says the merchandise is not good, do not buy it.</u>

Plan for the Future by Saving Now

Don't ever throw away anything that might come in handy later, like:

(1) ribbon and wrapping paper from gifts you receive
(2) brown paper bags from the A & P
(3) used aluminum foil
(4) corrugated cardboard packing inserts
(5) excelsior
(6) rags
(7) applesauce jars
(8) soup cans
(9) mailing tubes
(10) any kind of string

Store these things in appropriately marked bags or boxes for future use. Then, every six months or so, have a thorough house-cleaning, say it is cheaper to buy new things than to use up valuable space storing old ones, and throw out everything, including a lot of valuable papers belonging to your husband Al.

Making Old Clothes Do

Wherever possible, make old clothes do the job of new ones. Old clothes are more substantial than new ones anyway, because in the old days they made a thing to last. Be an example to your family in this area. Be certain, of course, that they are aware of your sacrifices:

"Well, I'm glad to say I won't be needing a new winter coat this year after all."

"Oh? How's that, Sylvia?"

"I glued the Woman's Section of the Sunday paper inside the lining of my old one, and now it's warm as toast."

If this has not left the desired impression, follow it up a few days later with a seeming contradiction:

"Well, I finally broke down and did it. I bought something for myself."

"Good. What did you buy, Sylvia?"

"I hated to spend the money, believe me, but today I bought a small roll of Scotch tape to hold my stockings together."

Make a list of all nieces, nephews and cousins who are older than your children and who are apt to outgrow their clothes before wearing them out. If your children object to wearing these hand-me-downs—if, for example, your son should show little enthusiasm for his cousin Sophie's sweaters or mittens—point out how thrilled a child in Europe would be to wear something as nice as that.

How To Buy New Clothes

Should no hand-me-downs be available, then you will have to think about buying new clothes at a regular store. If no one in your family is in the garment business, ask your druggist or the vegetable man to suggest the name of a store he's heard of. There's no point in going to a store that does not have a strong recommendation.

When you take your child to the store, keep these important points in mind:

(1) Never buy a color that will show the dirt.
(2) Never buy a fabric that will wear out.
(3) Never buy a style that is apt to change.

(4) Never buy a garment that fits—it should always be two or three sizes too large so that the child can grow into it.[8]

The most efficient way to buy clothes for any child below the age of twenty-two is to utilize him merely as a dressmaker's dummy and to address all questions about the fit or the appearance of the garment directly to the salesman:[9]

"Tell me, how does it fit in the crotch?"
"It looks pretty good from here, ma'am."

Should the child object to any garment that has been selected for him, ask the salesman if <u>he</u> talked to <u>his</u> mother like that when <u>he</u> was a boy. Never fear. The salesman will not let you down.

[8]The child should never be allowed to feel he looks well dressed.
[9]See THE THIRD PERSON INVISIBLE, Page 70.

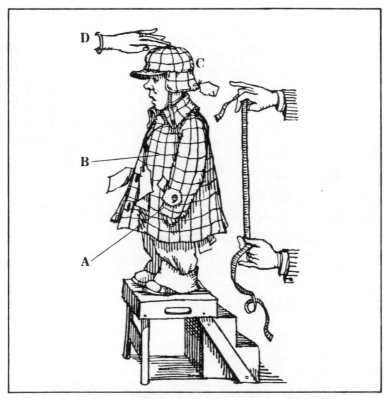

FIG. VIII : PROPER NEW CLOTHES TECHNIQUE FOR SON AGED 7 TO 22.

(A) Enough length in sleeve to cover second knuckle. **(B)** Enough room in chest to permit wearing a couple sweaters or a little fattening up. **(C)** Enough room in hat to permit growth between haircuts. **(D)** Steadying hand to prevent falling and soiling new clothes.

Quiz

Which of the following items should be saved and which thrown out? Check the appropriate boxes:

(1) Old apple cores

☐ Save
☐ Throw out

(2) Empty Bufferin bottles

☐ Save
☐ Throw out

(3) Empty aspirin tins

☐ Save
☐ Throw out

(4) Used paper napkins

☐ Save
☐ Throw out

(5) Used dental floss

☐ Save
☐ Throw out

Answers

(1) Save; you could make applesauce.
(2) Save; you may buy Bufferin some day when they'll be out of bottles.
(3) Save; you could keep parts of old wristwatches in them.
(4) Save; you could launder and re-use.
(5) Save; you could use for sewing on buttons.

When you feel you have mastered the area of Thrift, you may proceed to the next chapter on Education.

VI.
The Jewish Mother's Guide to Education

When your son is about to graduate from high school, go to him, put your hands on both his shoulders, smile proudly, and say as follows:

"Marvin?"

"Yeah?"

"Your father and I have been talking."

"Yeah?"

"We have come to a very important decision."

"Yeah?"

"We have decided that you are no longer a baby. I mean, after all, you're graduating high school and pretty soon now you will have to decide what you want to do in life."

"Yeah?"

"I just wanted to tell you that your

father and I have decided not to interfere. We have decided to let you do whatever you want to do, if you really want to do it. Whatever you want to do will be perfectly all right with us, so long as it makes you happy. You could be even a, a blacksmith, if that is what would make you happy. The only important thing, after all, is that you should do what makes you happy."

"O.K."

"Your father and I think, though, that you would be happiest if you would become a doctor, a lawyer, or a C.P.A."

Practice Drill

Pretend that the living room armchair is your son on the day he is to receive his law degree. Go around the back of the chair, place your hands on both sides and say in your Basic Tone of Voice:

"We want you to know we are very proud of you today, Marvin. Very proud. The only thing is, I thought I should tell you Papa's very hurt that you don't want to go into the button business with him."

Test Question

If your son should study medicine, law or accounting, then what should your daughter study?

Answer

Ballet, French, tap dancing, piano, and anything else that will enable her to meet a nice young man.

Now that you know how to cope with the area of Education, you are ready to tackle The Child Who Wants To Leave Home.

VII.
The Jewish Mother's Guide to Children Leaving Home

Sooner or later, to go to a fine university or to accept an attractive position with an out-of-town firm, one of your children may ask to leave the home.

Computing Maximum Allowable Distance

How many miles away should you allow your child to move? To compute the Maximum Allowable Distance, or M.A.D., multiply the speed in miles per hour of existing transportation to the new location by the amount of time in hours it takes for a frozen lambchop to defrost in your purse; or:

DISTANCE = M.P.H. x LAMBCHOP DEFROSTING TIME

The First Visit

As soon as possible after the child has moved into his new apartment, pay him a visit and do the following:

(1) Bring food. He probably does not know where to buy any in a strange city and is starving. Tell him how thin he looks.

(2) Take everything off his shelves and out of his drawers and line them with oilcloth.

(3) Wash his floor.

(4) Rearrange his furniture and buy plastic slipcovers for everything.

(5) Go out and get him a warm sweater, a pair of galoshes, a pair of gloves, a hat and (if the temperature there ever falls below 50° Fahrenheit) earmuffs.

(6) If he has plastic dinner plates, say he needs something more substantial and buy him china ones. If he has china ones, say he needs something more functional and buy him plastic ones.

After you have returned home, you may call up his professor or his employer, introduce yourself, tell him how tired your son looked to you when you saw him and suggest that he not be made to work so hard.

FIG. IX: PROPER OUTFIT FOR PNEUMONIA WEATHER (BELOW 50° F.)

Test Problem

Your son has been offered a job in a New York advertising agency. New York is 150 miles away. The train to New York travels at the rate of 75 miles per hour. A lambchop defrosts completely in the average purse in 2 hours. Should you allow your son to take this job?

Solution

No. What kind of a life is this, to work in an advertising agency? Feh!

Now that you have mastered The Child Who Wants To Leave Home, you may proceed to learn about Sex and Marriage.

VIII.
The Jewish Mother's Guide to Sex and Marriage

There are only two things a Jewish Mother needs to know about sex and marriage:
(1) Who is having sex?
(2) Why aren't they married?
Since it is by now apparent that everyone in the world is determined to have <u>some</u> kind of sex, it will therefore be your duty to make sure that everyone in the world gets married. And what more logical place to start than in your own home?

The Son:
The Early Years

It is never too early to begin preparing your son for marriage. At the age of eight or nine, start to develop in him an appreciation for the good grooming habits which will help him to win the hand of a capable young woman in marriage:

> "Feh! Look at your ears—what girl in her right mind would ever marry a boy that has wax in his ears?"

Develop his poise in a similar manner:

> "Stand up straight and don't slouch—what girl in her right mind is going to marry a hunchback?"[10]

The First Encounter

By age twelve or thirteen the child is ready for his first social encounter with the opposite sex. Arrange a party for Young People at your home or take the child to a dance.

If he appears hesitant to meet the young ladies, steer him over to several of them and urge him under your breath, or in audible whispers from a few paces off, to introduce himself. If he remains reticent, smoothe the way over those first few embarrassing moments by introducing him yourself:

> "This is my son Marvin who stands like a hunchback."

[10]You need not necessarily limit these tips to your own children. A child in the street should be supervised with the same loving care which you extend to your own: "Little boy, don't slouch. You want to make yourself a cripple?"

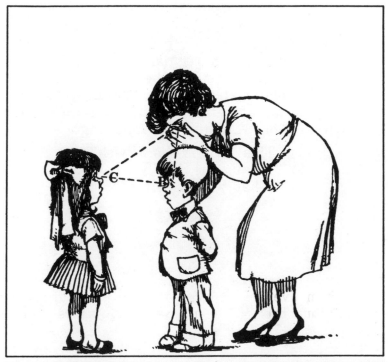

FIG. X: PROPER COACHING POSITION AT SON'S FIRST SOCIAL ENCOUNTER WITH OPPOSITE SEX.

Important: For optimum effectiveness in coaching and interpreting capacities, your Head (A) should form Right Triangle as above with heads of Son (B) and Small Female Child (C).

The High School Phase

By the time your son gets into high school, he will be going out on regular dates and will very likely insist on selecting the girls himself from among his classmates. Do not discourage this, but try to find out something about these girls for his own protection. Ask him the following:

      (1) "This girl, is she Jewish?"
      (2) "What's the family's name?"
      (3) "What was it before?"

The College Phase

By now your son is in college and dating quite seriously. If he is no longer living at home, your task will admittedly be more difficult, but by no means impossible. You will still arrange to spend vacations together, and you will still have the telephone and the U.S. Mails at your disposal.

FIG. XI: PROPER REACTION TO COMMAND "DON'T SLOUCH".

KEY: _ _ _ _ _ _ Slouch lines

_____ Good posture lines

Your son will probably have a young lady friend whom he particularly admires. As before, be sure of her background, but now the questioning should be on a more sophisticated level:

(1) "This girl, is she Jewish?"

(2) "She gets good marks in school?"

(3) "She smokes cigarettes in moderation?"

(4) "She drinks liquor in moderation?"

(5) "What kind of a girl smokes cigarettes and drinks liquor?"

Dinner With The Girl Friend

Invite your son's girl friend to your home for dinner so you will have a chance to determine whether she is good daughter-in-law material. To permit a completely objective evaluation, never speak to the young lady directly, but use your son as an intermediary:

"Does she like mashed potatoes?"

This form of address is known as The Third Person Invisible. Should your son ever decide to marry the girl, this device adapts very nicely to Basic Daughter-in-Law Technique, otherwise known as The I-Forget-Her-Name Gambit:

> "Is what's-her-name—is your wife coming over also?"

One word of warning: Should you for any reason disapprove of this young lady, take great pains to keep this fact from your son. Many young people today consider parental disapproval to be sufficient basis for marriage.

The Post-Graduate Period

If, by the time your son is out of college, he is still not married and he is not, God forbid, a homosexual, you must begin to Take Steps.

Speak to friends of yours who have daughters his age or maybe a few years older or a few years younger, and try to get the young people together. Pass the word around that your son, though a talented, intelligent and capable young man, is unable to find a girl who will go out with him.

Have your friends ask him regularly why a nice boy like that is not married.

Also speak of the matter to your son. Perhaps the idea of marriage has merely slipped his mind. Remind him. Often.

Joke about it in public to show that you aren't taking the matter too seriously:

"Excuse me. Mister."

"You talking to me, lady?"

"This is my son, Marvin."

"So?"

"Twenty-five years old. A Master's Degree in Romance Languages.[11] A careful driver. Tell me something confidentially."

"Yeah?"

"Would any young lady give her right arm to have a wonderful young man like that for a husband?"

"Search me, lady."

"Yes or no?"

"I suppose yes."

"Marvin, did you hear? Listen what the man is telling you."

[11] Optional Additional Comment: "It's only a shame he can't use all his romantic language to find himself a wife."

How to Act When He Finally Becomes Engaged

Suddenly, one day your son brings a strange girl over to the house and introduces her as his fianceé. What do you do?

You say hello to her, ask her what the weather is getting to be like outside, excuse yourself for a moment, lead your son off to a corner of the room, begin to sew a button on the sleeve of the coat he is wearing, and say to him as follows:

"Marvin. You intend to marry this girl?"

"Yeah. Not so loud, Ma."

"She's very pretty, Marvin."

"Yeah. Look, it's not very polite to—"

"Maybe even a little too pretty, you know what I mean?"

"Ma, look—"

"I hardly know what to tell you. (PAUSE. FINISH SEWING THE BUTTON, BEGIN TO BITE OFF THE THREAD, STOP, STUDY THE END OF IT AND LOOK UP INTO HIS FACE) Look, you're still so young. You know what I mean? What's your big hurry to get married all of a sudden?"

Test Problem

Using The Neighbor's-Model-Child Gambit, how would you convince your son to get married?

Solution

Say to him:
"So how come Naomi's boy is already married and he's three years younger?"

You have now done all you can be expected to do for your Son. It is time to give some thought to your Daughter.

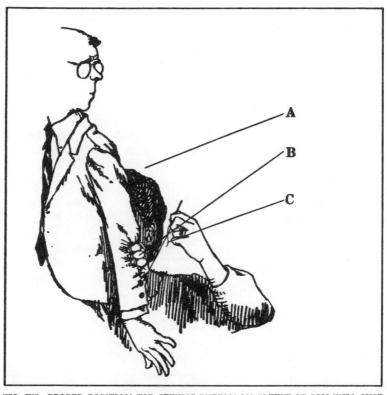

FIG. XII : PROPER POSITION FOR SEWING BUTTON ON SLEEVE OF SON WHO JUST ANNOUNCED HE IS ENGAGED TO BE MARRIED.

(A) Head shielded from view of son's fianceé to mask whispered remarks. **(B)** Grip on arm itself rather than sleeve. **(C)** Thread is minimum 180 lb. test.

The Daughter:
What to Do Before the Date
(High School & College Phases)

If you have a daughter, you are fortunate in that you will be able to meet and personally evaluate all the young men who come to the house to take her away.

Make sure your husband[12] is wearing a shirt when the young man rings the bell. Greet the young man at the door. Appraise him closely from head to foot. Ask him the following:

> (1) "You're Jewish?"
> (2) "What's your family's name?"
> (3) "What was it before?"

If the young man is driving a car, be sure and add these important queries:

> (1) "You know how to drive?"
> (2) "You have a driver's license?"
> (3) "How fast do you drive?"
> (4) "Your father knows you're out?"

Even if the young man has answered all your questions in a satisfactory manner, it is not a bad idea to frown, avert your head and sigh:

[12]He's the one in the undershirt watching television.

"Ach, I don't like it, I tell you. You youngsters all drive like maniacs. You'll wind up in some ditch tonight, mark my words. (PAUSE. SMILE, FROWNING) All right, all right—go, drive careful, and have a wonderful time. And I'm going to worry myself sick about you, I promise you."

As they are about to go out the door, turn to your daughter and whisper loudly in her ear:

"Stay all the way on the right side of the seat, if you know what's good for you."

The Post-Graduate Phase

If your daughter should not be married by the time she is out of college, apply the same tactics to her as to your son, with these subtle variations:

Seek out any young man at a party or other social gathering and begin to sell him on your daughter. Speak of her excellent disposition. Point out her many physical attributes:

"A face like a Vermeer—you know Vermeer?"

"Yes, the painter."

"She won the Queen Esther contest when she was five."

"You don't say."

"She has natural curly hair, maybe you noticed."

"Oh yes, well—"

"And teeth? Did you see how straight her teeth are?"

"Well, as a matter of —"

"Three thousand dollars I spent having her teeth straightened—four years at the orthodontist's so her mouth could close."

"Look, I really have to be —"

"A beautiful girl. Beautiful. (PAUSE) The only thing, she is maybe a tiny bit heavy in the bust. (SMILE) It runs in the family."

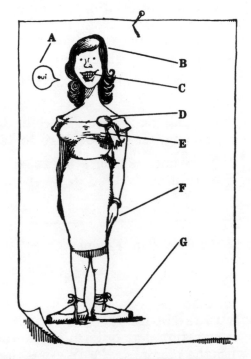

FIG. XIII: CHART FOR POINTING OUT DAUGHTER'S ATTRIBUTES.

(A) Speaks a fluent French. (B) Has natural curly hair. (C) Had natural curly teeth straightened. (D) Won 1st prize in the Queen Esther Contest. (E) Is maybe a tiny bit heavy in the bust (it runs in the family). (F) Has strong, capable hands for cooking, cleaning and sewing. (G) Since the age of 3, dances ballet like a regular Pavlov.

Calling attention to a slight imperfection often lends just the right note of credibility to your sales pitch. In any case, do not beat around the bush. The young man will appreciate your frankness. Be direct. Beg him to invite your daughter out—

"For a malted milkshake, I'll pay for it myself."

Should the young man actually come to the house to take your daughter out, be sure to reassure him:

"You're not making a mistake, believe me. She refuses forty dates a week."

Dinner With The Boy Friend

As soon as you can swing it, invite the young man over to the house for dinner. Spend the whole day in preparation, but only allow your daughter to assist with the menial tasks like peeling the onions.

At the dinner table, make constant reference to the delicious and nourishing quality of the food, and be sure to stress who prepared it:

"I want you should know my daughter cooked every bit of it—she wouldn't even let me in the kitchen."

This is an ideal occasion to bring up your daughter's cultural background:

"Piano lessons we gave her, ballet, tap dancing, interpretive dancing, baton twirling. She draws, she paints, she sculpts, she speaks a fluent French. Say something in French, precious. (PAUSE) What, already you forgot?"

Point out that a good cultural background makes for compatability, which is more important in a marriage than romance:

"Listen, you'll come down off your cloud, this way you'll have a basis. You'll speak French together, you'll play the piano together, you'll dance ballet together —you'll have a basis."

How To Behave When You Discover Your Daughter Necking In The Living Room

Wait until the young man has gone home, go in to your daughter's room and say to her as follows:

"Miriam."

"Oh, hi Ma."

"Miriam, I saw. I saw what you were doing in there."

"Oh."

"Miriam, who taught you this?"

"Oh, for God's sake, Ma. I'm a big girl now."

"Miriam, we are decent people. We have always tried to teach you the right thing. How could you do this to us?"

"Ma, for God's sake, I was only kissing—"

"Do you know what your father will do when I'll tell him? Do you?"

"No, but—"

"He will have a heart attack, that's what he will do. I promise you."

"Look, Ma, you don't have to tell—"

"Not only that, just think what the neighbors would say if they knew."

"Look—"

FIG. XIV: PROPER VISUALIZATION OF DAUGHTER AFTER SHE IS FOUND NECKING IN THE LIVING ROOM.

"For this I had to have your teeth straightened? For this I bought you contact lenses? For this I paid good money to have them teach you how to speak French?"

"Ma—"

"Ach, I don't know what to do with you. (PAUSE) My own daughter, a streetwalker. (PAUSE) If you have any consideration for your parents at all, you'll do the only decent thing."

"What's that?"

"You'll leave this house and you'll not come back until you're a virgin."

The Last Resort

Your daughter has spent a final fruitless summer in the Catskills or Palm Springs or Fort Lauderdale, she is over twenty-five years of age and—God forbid—she still has no serious prospects for marriage at all. What must be done?

(1) Think it over calmly.
(2) Consider all the angles.
(3) Weigh all the alternatives.
(4) Panic.

Go to your daughter, assume the Basic Facial Expression and the Basic Tone of Voice and deliver this final memorized address:

"I want to tell you something very important."

"What?"

"I have tried to be a good mother to you, I suppose I have failed."

"Oh God."

"God knows how I've suffered to bring you up properly, to teach you to take proper care of yourself, to stand up straight—don't slouch when I'm talking to you—to give you nice clothes to wear, to give you a decent education. What do I ask in return —gratitude? Listen, gratitude I can do without, and I wouldn't get it anyway, you know it and so do I."

"Ma, for God's—"

"O.K., O.K., I'm not complaining. All I'm saying is this: I'm not getting any younger. I would like to know before I die that you are married and happy and not alone in the world. I would, believe me, go into the coffin with a smile on my face to have seen and held on my lap a couple of grandchildren."

"What am I supposed to—"

"All right, look. I know you've tried. I'm not saying that. The thing is, maybe I've been too critical of the young men you've gone out with. (TO CEILING): Is it a sin to want only the best for your children? (TO DAUGHTER): What I am saying is this: Maybe it's not so important you should marry only a professional man. Your father, after all, was in ladies' buttons. So keep looking around, and if you should come across a nice young fellow and you should fall in love with him, and if he should also be in love with you, and if—may the good Lord not burn out my tongue from my mouth for saying this— if this young man should not be a college graduate . . . all right—I say all right, go ahead and marry him! (PAUSE. SOFTLY): By that time, your father and I will probably both be dead anyway."

Test Problem

Using The Neighbor's-Model-Child Gambit, how would you convince your daughter to get married?

Solution

Say to her:

"So how come Naomi's girl, who is three years younger and believe me no beauty, is already not only married but has two children and a station wagon?"

If you have been successful in the area of Sex and Marriage, you will find the next short chapter very useful.

IX.
How to be a Jewish Grandmother

An exhaustive study of this area is currently in progress. Until all the research has been completed and the findings tabulated, here are a few Basic Remarks About The Baby For Friends which should carry you through the first few critical months of grandmotherhood:

(1) "They don't give him enough food."

(2) "He looks exactly like Miriam when she was a baby."

(3) "They don't give him enough fresh air."

(4) "He looks exactly like his Aunt Gertrude."

(5) "They don't give him enough rest."

(6) "He looks exactly like old man Finklestein."

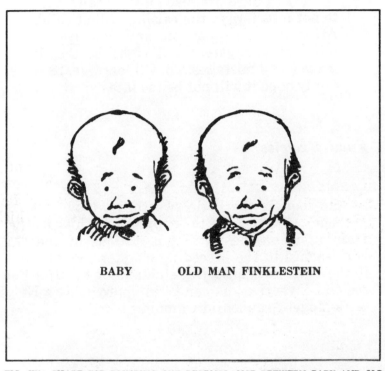

BABY   **OLD MAN FINKLESTEIN**

FIG. XV: CHART FOR POINTING OUT RESEMBLANCE BETWEEN BABY AND OLD
MAN FINKLESTEIN.

(7) "They don't give him enough attention."

(8) "I have promised myself faithfully to not interfere in the raising of that child. After all, he's their son, and they are intelligent youngsters. All right, so they'll make a few mistakes. They'll learn. (PAUSE) I only hope it will not be too late."

Final Exercise

As soon as the little sweetheart is able to comprehend you, begin to supplement his mother's training techniques with adaptations of the skills you learned in the preceding chapters. For example, if the child seems at all reluctant to Eat His Food, see how inventive you can be in improvising a Neighbor's-Model-Grandchild Gambit.

(NOTE: For a helpful explanation of some of the technical terms used in this text, you may consult the following comprehensive Glossary.)

Glossary of Terms

a nice boy:
A young man who owns his own car.

a good boy:
A young man who owns his own car and brings his date's mother candy.

a fine boy:
A young man who owns his own car, brings his date's mother candy, and studies medicine.

basis:
(As in "With her you would have a real <u>basis</u> for a marriage") She sculpts, but she is ugly.

bum:
A young man who does not call for a girl at her home but arranges to meet her somewhere.

bathing:
Swimming.

capable:
   (As in "She's a very capable girl") She's an excellent cook, but she is ugly.

chorus girl:
   Anyone who wears too much makeup.

complaining:
   What a Jewish Mother is not doing.

coronary:
   Upper middle class heart attack.

Cousins Club:
   All the relatives get together on a Sunday night, smoke cigars, play gin rummy and complain.

culture:
   (Active mood) Playing a musical instrument, painting a picture, writing a play, speaking a foreign language other than Yiddish.
   (Passive mood) Knowing somebody who plays a musical instrument, paints pictures, writes plays, speaks a foreign language other than Yiddish.

disposition:
(As in "She has an excellent disposition") She does not bite, but she is still ugly.

drunkard:
Anybody who accepts your offer of an alcoholic beverage.

feh!:
Fie!

foolishness:
Anything not directly related to the care of the family, the household or a profession.

for later:
(As in "Take a little spongecake for later") To be eaten within the next two weeks.

goniff:
Rascal; ruffian; reprobate; rotter; (See "roughneck").

gratitude:
What a Jewish Mother does not expect.

heart attack:
Lower middle class coronary.

hunchback:
Anybody who does not stand up as straight as a Marine recruit.

makes a living:
He could support a wife and a couple of children.

makes a nice appearance:
He wears a double breasted suit.

nourishing:
Fattening.

pig:
Anyone who does not take small bites when eating.

poison:
What a Jewish Mother is not trying to feed you.

properly:
Just as you're told.

roughneck:
Anybody who talks back to his mother or does not wash properly behind the ears.

scarecrow:
   Anybody who weighs less than 250 lbs.

sensible:
   Out of fashion.

shameful waste:
   Throwing out a teabag after using it only once.

sliver:
   Any portion of food smaller than a breadbox.

substantial:
   Wealthy.

swimming:
   Bathing.

The Evil Eye:
   What you should not know from.

The Outside:
   The Great Unknown; anything not in the home.

tramp:
   Feminine of "bum"; any girl who lets a boy kiss her on the mouth.

tube:
   What they will have to feed you through if you don't eat properly.

unmarried surgeon:
The answer to a mother's prayer.

wash down:
(As in "Take a little bread to <u>wash down</u> the spongecake") To keep it company in your stomach.

younger:
What a Jewish Mother is not getting any.

Please turn the page for a final message from the one person who made this entire study possible.

The Last Word by the Author's Mother

So you've read his book and, God willing, enjoyed it.* Do I have to tell you how proud a mother would be of a son like that? I don't. Now maybe he'll give up all this foolishness and go into a worthwhile profession.

*Believe me, I wouldn't spoil your fun for a minute, but if you had not spent the money on this book and sent it instead to Asia, a needy child could have had six nourishing meals.

DAN GREENBURG grew up in Chicago, studied art at the University of Illinois, received a Master of Arts in Industrial Design at U.C.L.A., and then threw a wonderful education right out the window and became a writer. Since then he has written numerous books, including HOW TO MAKE YOUR SELF MISERABLE, JUMBO THE BOY & ARNOLD THE ELEPHANT (a juvenile), CHEWSDAY PHILLY, PORNO-GRAPHICS, SCORING and SOMETHING'S THERE. His two one-act plays, ARF and THE GREAT AIRPLANE SNATCH, have been produced Off-Broadway and he was also a contributor to OH, CALCUTTA. He has written several screenplays and contributed articles to numerous national magazines. Though 39 years old, he still does not know how to stand up straight or to eat properly.

This book is published by

PRICE/STERN/SLOAN
Publishers, Inc., Los Angeles

whose other splendid titles include such literary classics as:

HOW TO BE AN ITALIAN
CHOPPED-UP CHINESE
YOU WERE BORN ON A ROTTEN DAY
"THE PROFIT" BY KEHLOG ALBRAN
THE VERY IMPORTANT PERSON NOTEBOOK
SELF ANALYSIS
and many, many more

They are available wherever books are sold or may be ordered
directly from the publisher. For complete list,
send a *stamped, self-addressed* envelope to:

PRICE/STERN/SLOAN
Publishers, Inc., Los Angeles

410 North La Cienega Boulevard
Los Angeles, California 90048

PRICE/STERN/SLOAN
Publishers, Inc., Los Angeles